Contents

Acknowledgements

I am very grateful to all the schools, institutions, teachers and students around the world who either piloted or commented on the material:

Maria Heloísa Aldino, São Paulo, Brazil
Graham Bathgate, Tokyo, Japan
Paloma Campomanes, Valencia, Spain
Ian Chitty, Cambridge, UK
Rosa Currás, Valencia, Spain
Marek Doskocz, Warsaw, Poland
Ludmila Gorodetskaya, Moscow, Russia
John Irving, Colchester, UK
Roy Kingsbury, UK
Elisabeth de Lange, Beckum, Germany
Agnieszka Lenko-Szymanska, Lodz, Poland
Ricky Lowes, London, UK
David Perry, Valencia, Spain
Tony Robinson, Cambridge, UK
Olga Vinogradova, Moscow, Russia
Shu-Hui Wang, Taiwan

I would particularly like to thank Nóirín Burke and Martine Walsh at Cambridge University Press for all their help, guidance and support during the writing of this series.
My thanks also to Liz Driscoll for her experienced editing of the material and to Jo Barker and Sarah Warburton for their excellent design and artwork.

Vocabulary
in practice 1

30 units of
self-study
vocabulary
exercises

Glennis Pye

with tests

CAMBRIDGE
UNIVERSITY PRESS

PUBLISHED BY THE PRESS SYNDICATE OF THE UNIVERSITY OF CAMBRIDGE
The Pitt Building, Trumpington Street, Cambridge, United Kingdom

CAMBRIDGE UNIVERSITY PRESS
The Edinburgh Building, Cambridge CB2 2RU, UK
40 West 20th Street, New York, NY 10011–4211, USA
477 Williamstown Road, Port Melbourne, VIC 3207, Australia
Ruiz de Alarcón 13, 28014 Madrid, Spain
Dock House, The Waterfront, Cape Town 8001, South Africa

http://www.cambridge.org

First published 2002
Third printing 2003

Printed in Italy by G. Canale & C. S.p.A

Typeface Bembo 10/11pt   *System* QuarkXpress®   [HMCL]

A Catalogue record for this book is available at the British Library

ISBN 0 521 01080 2

To the student

This book will give you the chance to practise your vocabulary in a fun way.

Vocabulary in Practice 1 has:
- 30 units of short, enjoyable exercises – each unit practises groups of words which belong together
- 3 Tests – one after every 10 units, helping you to remember the words from those units
- an Answer Key
- a Word List – this is a list of all the words in each unit with information about how the words are used.

You can use the book in two ways:
1 Start at the beginning of the book. Do units 1–30 and then do the Tests.
2 Look at the Contents. Do the units you think are important first. When you have finished the book, do the Tests.

You can do each unit in two ways:
1 Do the unit and check your answers in the Answer Key. Study the Word List and learn the words you got wrong. Then do the exercise again.
2 Study the Word List for the unit. Then do the unit and check your answers.

Note Do the exercises in this book in pencil. Then you can do the exercises again after a week or a month. Repeating the exercises will help you to remember the words.

Here are some ideas to help you to learn vocabulary:
- Learn groups of words which belong together [e.g. skirt, coat, trousers, etc.].
- Learn a word and also its opposite [e.g. beautiful/ugly, hot/cold].
- Draw pictures: some words are easier to remember if you draw a picture and write the word under it, e.g.

hand

spoon

fish

- Write new words in a notebook: write the meaning in English or in your own language, then write a sentence using the word.

I hope you find this book useful and that it makes learning English words fun.

1 Your body

A Circle the correct word in each pair.

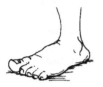

1 (foot) / hair   **2** eye / neck   **3** head / mouth   **4** leg / toe

5 face / finger   **6** ear / hand   **7** arm / nose

B Label the pictures with the other words from A.

1   *finger*

2

3

4

5

6

7

  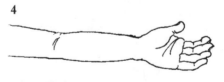 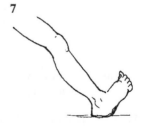

2 Clothes

A Complete the words.

1 Mike's at work. He's wearing t*rousers*, a s___t, a j____t and s___s.
2 Judith isn't at work today. She's wearing j___s and a T-s___t.
3 Elena's in the office. She's wearing a s___t and a j____r.
4 It's a very cold day. Eric's wearing a s___f, a h_t, g____s and a c__t.
5 Julia's at a party. She's wearing a d___s.

B Complete the crossword.

		¹j	e	a	n	²s			
³									
			⁴				⁵		
⁶						⁷			

1 something you wear on your legs that are usually blue
2 something you wear on your feet
3 something you wear on top of your other clothes when you go out
4 something you wear on your hands when it's cold
5 something you wear round your neck when it's cold
6 something you wear on your legs
7 something you wear on your head when it's cold

3 Describing character

A Complete the sentences with the words in the box.

boring ~~clever~~ friendly funny
lazy naughty shy stupid unkind

1 Alsana's a .....*clever*..... person.

2 Richard's a .... person.

3 Terry's a................. person.

4 Jan's a .... person.

5 Ben's an .... person.

6 Neil's a .... person.

7 Betty's a .... person.

8 Mike's a .... person.

9 Gemma's a .... person.

1 I can speak six languages.

2 I like relaxing all day and watching TV.

3 2 + 2 = 5, I think.

4 I laugh a lot when I'm with you, Jan.

5 I'm not helping her!

6 I'm not very good at talking to new people.

7 Hi, my name's Betty. What's your name?

8 People say I'm not very interesting.

9 Look! I'm drawing on the wall.

B Join the words with opposite meanings.

1 clever   good

2 friendly   kind

3 naughty   stupid

4 unkind   unfriendly

4 Describing appearance

A Join the words with opposite meanings.

1 beautiful   tall
2 fat   thin
3 handsome   ugly
4 old   ugly
5 short   young

B Complete the sentences with words from A.

1 He's an .... *old* ....man. He's 92.

2 He eats too much. That's why he's ....

3 She's only ten years old. She's too .... to buy cigarettes.

4 She's very .... She's 1m 84.

5 She's very .... All the men love her.

6 She wants to be a model, but at 1m 50 she's too ....

7 All my friends have his picture on their walls – they think he's so

....

8 I don't understand why they like him – I think he's ....

C Complete the words.

1 Lucy's got l.ou.g hair.

2 Nasser's got s___t hair.

3 David's got c___y hair.

4 Sarah's got s_____t hair.

5 How you feel

A The <u>underlined</u> words are in the wrong sentences. Write the correct word for each sentence.

1 I don't sleep much at night, so I'm really <u>cold</u>.   ....*tired*....

2 I'm <u>hungry</u>. I need a drink.   ....

3 He has a very high temperature. I think he's <u>tired</u>.   ....

4 I'm really <u>ill</u> in the evening because I don't eat much at work.   ....

5 If you feel <u>thirsty</u>, why don't you put a jumper on?   ....

6 He's <u>hot</u> again and is coming home from hospital soon.   ....

7 Take your coat off. You must be really <u>well</u> in here.   ....

B Complete the sentences with the words in the box.

1
Great! A party invitation!

| angry bored frightened |
| ~~happy~~ sad |

He's ....*happy*.... .

2
It's dark and I'm alone.

She's ....

3
My toy's broken.

He's ....

4
I can't think of anything to do.

He's ....

5
You're wearing my new T-shirt.

She's ....

C Complete the sentences with the words from B.

1 Take a book with you so you don't get ....*bored*.... while you're waiting.

2 She's .... because her best friend can't come to her party.

3 Little children are sometimes .... of the dark.

4 I'm .... because I don't have to go to work today.

5 You can see he's .... He's very red in the face.

6 The family

A Put the words in the box into the correct group.

~~brother~~ ~~daughter~~ father granddaughter grandfather
grandmother grandson husband mother sister son wife

women: *daughter*

men: *brother*

B Look at the family tree and complete the sentences with the words from A.

1 Alice is Bill's .... *wife* ....

2 Kelly is Alice and Bill's ....

3 Robert is Elena's ....

4 Elena is Nick's ....

5 Bill is Nick and Elena's ....

6 Liam is Kelly's ....

7 Alice is Kelly and Liam's ....

8 Liam is Alice and Bill's ....

9 Liam is Elena and Robert's ....

10 Elena is Kelly and Liam's ....

11 Bill is Kelly and Liam's ....

12 Kelly is Elena and Robert's ....

Alice   Bill

Nick   Elena   Robert

Kelly   Liam

C Complete what the people are saying with the words from A.

LIAM: 'My (1) ...*father*....'s name is Robert and my (2) ....'s name is Elena. I've got one (3) .... Her name is Kelly. My mother's got one (4) .... His name is Nick. My (5) .... is called Alice and my (6) .... is called Bill.'

BILL: 'My (7) ....'s name is Alice. We have a (8) .... called Elena and a (9) .... called Nick. Elena is married – her (10) ....'s name is Robert. We have a (11) .... called Kelly and a (12) .... called Liam.'

7 Countries

A Find the names of 20 countries in the grid. Then write the words in the correct group.

P	O	R	T	U	G	A	L	D	F	P	J	B
A	S	O	U	T	H	A	F	R	I	C	A	X
Y	I	A	R	G	E	N	T	I	N	A	P	R
A	N	I	K	G	E	R	M	A	N	Y	A	S
U	D	T	E	C	E	K	P	O	L	A	N	D
S	I	L	Y	B	Z	C	H	I	N	A	G	R
T	A	S	P	A	I	N	G	J	P	C	R	U
R	V	C	E	F	R	A	N	C	E	J	E	S
A	U	N	I	T	E	D	S	T	A	T	E	S
L	R	I	T	A	L	Y	L	X	N	F	C	I
I	V	C	A	N	A	D	A	O	Q	U	E	A
A	S	W	F	L	N	C	B	R	A	Z	I	L
U	N	I	T	E	D	K	I	N	G	D	O	M

Africa   _South Africa_

Asia   C_HINA_, I_NDIA_, J_APAN_

Australasia   A_USTRALIA_

Europe   F_RANCE_, G_ERMANY_, G_REECE_,
                     I_RELAND_, I_TALY_, P_OLAND_,
                     P_ORTUGAL_, R_USSIA_, S_PAIN_,
                     T_URKEY_, U_NITED KINGDOM_

North America   C_ANADA_, U_NITED STATES_

South America   A_RGENTINA_, B_RAZIL_

It is not possible to list all the countries of the world here. If your country is not in this list, please check its English name with your teacher or in a dictionary.

8 Nationalities and languages

A Complete each word in the *nationalities* column with one of the endings in the box. Then complete the *official languages* column.

| an | ian | ese | ench | ish | k |

countries	nationalities	official languages
1 Argentina	Argentin*ian*	*Spanish*
2 Australia	Austral*ian*	English
3 Brazil	Brazil*ian*	Portuguese
4 Canada	Canad*ian*	english + french
5 China	Chin*ese*	
6 France	Fr*ench*	
7 Germany	Germ*an*	
8 Greece	Gree*k*	Greek
9 India	Ind*ian*	
10 Ireland	Ir*ish*	
11 Italy	Ital*ian*	
12 Japan	Japan*ese*	
13 Poland	Pol*ish*	
14 Portugal	Portugu*ese*	
15 Russia	Russ*ian*	
16 South Africa	South Afric*an*	
17 Spain	Span*ish*	
18 Turkey	Turk*ish*	
19 United Kingdom	Brit*ish*	
20 United States	Americ*an*	

It is not possible to list all the countries of the world here. If your country is not in this list, please check its English name with your teacher or in a dictionary. Note also that in most countries there are other languages apart from the official ones.

9 Numbers

A How many birds are in each nest? Write the numbers and the words.

a ...3... *three*

b ... *two*

c ... *nine*

d ... *six*

e ... *zero*

f ... *four*

g ... *eight*

h ... *one*

i ... *ten*

j ... *five*

k ... *seven*

B Join the numbers and words. Then write them in order from smallest to biggest.

a 13   eighteen   ...11... *eleven*

b 20   eleven

c 17   fifteen

d 12   fourteen

e 11   nineteen

f 16   seventeen

g 19   sixteen

h 15   thirteen

i 18   twelve

j 14   twenty

C Answer the questions.

1 How many legs has a dog got?   It's got ...*four*... .

2 How many days are there in a week?   There are ... .

3 How many toes have you got?   I've got ... .

4 How many months are there in a year?   There are ... .

10 Colours

A What colour are the things in the pictures? Complete the crossword.

B Write colours for the numbers in the picture.

1 *yellow*
2 ....
3 ....
4 ....

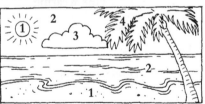

C Answer these questions.

1 What colour are your eyes?   They are ....

2 What colour is your favourite T-shirt?   It's ....

3 What colour is your coat?   It's ....

4 What colour is your favourite jumper?   It's ....

Test 1 (Units 1–10)

A What do you wear and where do you wear it? Complete the words.

1 You wear a h_a_t on your h_ead_ .

2 You wear a s____ around your n_eck_ .

3 You wear g_____ on your h____ .

4 You wear t_____ on your l___ .

5 You wear s____ on your f___ .

B Who are the people in Fred's family, what do they look like and what are they wearing? Complete the sentences.

1 Joanna is Fred's ....*mother*....... . She's ......*beautiful*...... .
   She's wearing a long ......*dress*...... .

2 Sylvia is Fred's .... She's ....
   She's wearing a .... and a ....

3 Ben is Fred's ....
   He's very .... He's wearing
   .... and a ....

4 Millie is Fred's ....
   She's .... She's wearing ....
   and a ....

Ben   Joanna

Sylvia

Fred   Millie

C What are these people like? Complete the sentences.

1 He never does any work. He's very ....

2 People laugh a lot when they're with her. She's very ....

3 He always helps people. He's very ....

4 He never helps people. He's very ....

5 She passes all her exams at school. She's very ....

6 He always talks about the same thing. He's very ....

D How do you feel? Complete the sentences.

1 I'm .... *hot* ....   Take your coat off, then.

2 I'm ....   Go to see the doctor, then.

3 I'm ....   Go to bed, then.

4 I'm ....   Try to think of something to do, then.

5 I'm ....   Have a drink, then.

6 Why are you running away?   Because I'm ....

E Complete the lists.

countries	nationalities
1 Argentina	....
2	French
3 Spain	....
4	Japanese
5 Germany	....
6	American
7 Portugal	....
8	Chinese

F Write the answers as words.

a $3 + 4 =$ .... *seven* ....

b $5 + 8 =$ ....

c $6 + 12 =$ ....

d $8 + 1 =$ ....

e $7 - 7 =$ ....

f $13 - 2 =$ ....

g $20 - 5 =$ ....

h $16 - 15 =$ ....

G True or false? If the sentence is false, write the correct colour.

1 Elephants are pink.   .... *false* .... *grey* ....

2 Bananas are red.   ....

3 Grass is orange.   ....

4 The sky is blue.   ....

5 The sea is red.   ....

6 Chocolate is brown.   ....

11 Months of the year

A Find the names of the 12 months of the year in the grid. Then complete the words in the list below.

J	A	N	U	A	R	Y	P	L	U	P	R
K	P	O	E	U	W	X	O	C	J	A	I
F	R	I	D	G	V	E	C	J	U	L	Y
U	I	N	D	U	R	S	T	P	N	C	S
D	L	F	O	S	I	R	O	V	E	N	M
E	S	E	P	T	E	M	B	E	R	O	B
R	I	B	M	S	J	O	E	L	Z	S	W
M	A	R	C	H	F	G	R	K	E	G	H
A	X	U	R	N	O	V	E	M	B	E	R
B	N	A	C	W	T	Y	Q	U	V	N	M
L	H	R	D	E	C	E	M	B	E	R	S
M	A	Y	R	G	J	I	M	B	S	R	E

1 J *anuary*
2 F
3 M
4 A
5 M
6 J
7 J
8 A
9 S
10 O
11 N
12 D

B When were these people born? Complete the sentences with the months.

1 Annabel: 19.11.1989   Annabel was born in ___*November*___ .

2 Liam: 17.10.1978   Liam was born in ___ .

3 Zoe: 22.1.1992   Zoe was born in ___ .

4 Ben: 21.12.1964   Ben was born in ___ .

5 Sasha: 19.2.1982   Sasha was born in ___ .

6 Henry: 30.9.1995   Henry was born in ___ .

7 James: 25.5.1970   James was born in ___ .

8 Harry: 29.6.1945   Harry was born in ___ .

9 Holly: 13.8.1998   Holly was born in ___ .

10 Ruby: 14.4.1957   Ruby was born in ___ .

11 Ella: 17.3.2000   Ella was born in ___ .

12 Joe: 27.7.1997   Joe was born in ___ .

12 Days of the week

A Complete the crossword with the words for the seven days of the week.

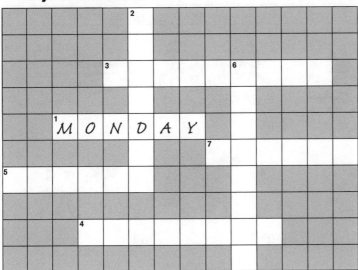

B Complete the sentences with the days of the week.

JUNE						
M	**T**	**W**	**T**	**F**	**S**	**S**
				1	2	3
4	5	6	7	8	9	10
11	12	13	14	15	16	17
18	19	20	21	22	23	24
25	26	27	28	29	30	

1 I'm going to the hairdresser's on _Thursday_ 7 June.

2 I'm going to Karen's party on .... 22 June.

3 I'm going to the dentist's on .... 11 June.

4 I'm going to the cinema on .... 27 June.

5 I'm going to Mum and Dad's on .... 10 June.

6 I'm going shopping with Polly on .... 19 June.

7 I'm going to Adam and Linda's wedding on .... 2 June.

13 The weather

A Complete the sentences with the words in the box.

| cloudy | cold | ~~foggy~~ | hot | raining | snowing | sunny | windy |

1 It's *foggy* .   **2** It's ....   **3** It's ....

4 It's ....   **5** It's ....   **6** It's ....

7 It's ....   **8** It's ....

B Complete the sentences with the words from A.

1 It's *foggy* .   **5** It's ....

2 It's ....   **6** It's ....

3 It's ....   **7** It's ....

4 It's ....   **8** It's ....

14 A house

A Look at the picture and complete the paragraph with the words in the box.

| bathroom | ~~bedrooms~~ | dining room | garden | hall | kitchen | living room |

This large house has two lovely (1) *bedrooms* and a (2) ....
with a bath and shower. Downstairs there is a very comfortable
(3) .... , a (4) .... , a large (5) .... and a
(6) .... with a door going out into a beautiful (7) ....

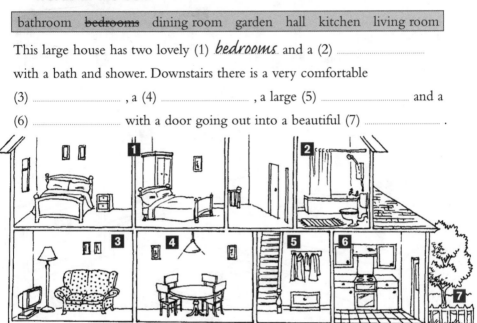

B Label the picture with the words in the box.

| door | floor | letterbox | ~~roof~~ | stairs | wall | window |

1 ....*roof*.............
2 ....
3 ....
4 ....
5 ....
6 ....
7 ....

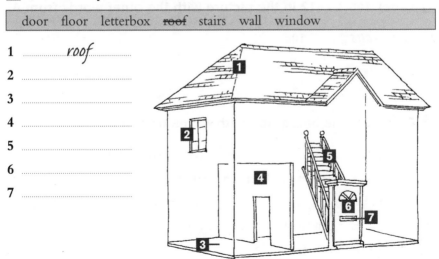

15 Living room

A Look at items 1–6 in the picture and circle the correct word in each pair.

1 (picture) / rug
2 light / video
3 curtains / cushions
4 CD player / TV
5 shelf / table
6 armchair / sofa

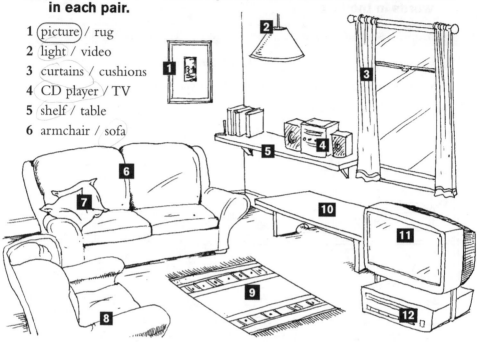

B Label items 7–12 in the picture with the other words from A.

7 cushions
8 armchaus
9 rug
10 table
11 Be TV
12 OVD players

C Complete the paragraph with words from A and B.

The living room is a small room with an (a) armchair and a
(b) sofa to sit on. There's a pretty (c) rug on
the floor and a (d) shelf to put books on. There's a
(e) pictures on the wall and some (f) cushions to
make the sofa more comfortable.

16 Kitchen

A Label the picture with the words in the box.

cooker   cupboard   ~~fridge~~   microwave   sink   washing machine

1 _fridge_   3 _cupboard_   5 _cooker_

2 _sink_   4 _washing m_   6 _microwave_

B Complete the crossword.

	¹g			²c	u	³p	
⁴p	l	a	t	e		a	
	a					n	
	s	⁵b		⁶k			
	⁷s	p	o	o	n		
		w		i			
		l		⁸f	o	r	k
				e			

1 something you drink orange juice out of
2 something you drink coffee out of
3 something you cook food in
4 something flat you put your food on
5 something you eat soup from
6 something you cut food with
7 something you eat soup with
8 something you eat peas and carrots with

17 Bathroom

A Label the picture with the words in the box.

| basin   bath   ~~mirror~~   shower   toilet |

1 *mirror*
2 *basin*
3 *toilet*
4 *bath*
5 *shower*

B Complete the words in the shopping list. Then join the words with the pictures.

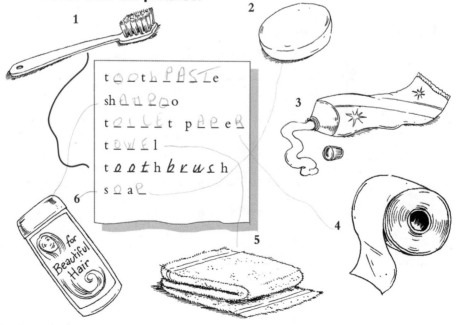

t o o t h P A S T e
sh a u p o o
t o i l e t   p a p e r
t o w e l
t o o t h b r u s h
s o a p

18 Bedroom

A Label the picture with the words in the box.

alarm clock   bed   chest of drawers   duvet
lamp   ~~pillow~~   sheet   wardrobe

1 _pillow_
2 _bed_
3 _sheet_
4 _duvet_
5 _alarm clock_
6 _lamp_
7 _chest of drawers_
8 _wardrobe_

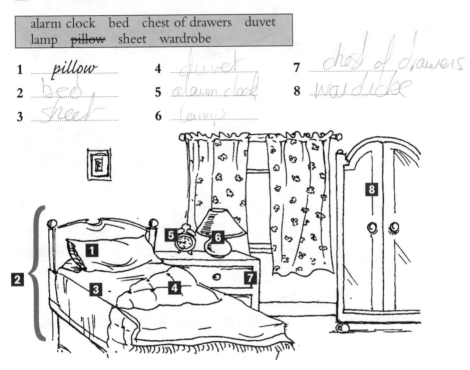

B Complete the paragraph with words from A.

Sam usually goes upstairs to his bedroom at about ten o'clock. He puts on
the small (a) _lamp_ next to his bed. He takes his trousers off,
opens the (b) _wardrobe_ door and puts them in. He puts his
pyjamas on. He gets into (c) _bed_ , pulls the (d) _duvet_
over himself, puts his head on the (e) _pillow_ and goes to sleep.
In the morning the (f) _alarm clock_ wakes him up at
seven o'clock.

19 Travel

A Complete the words.

1 c _a_ r
2 t _r_ _a_ _i_ n
3 b _u_ s
4 p _l_ _a_ _n_ e
5 h _e_ _l_ _i_ _c_ _o_ _p_ _t_ e r
6 b _i_ _k_ e
7 m _o_ _t_ _o_ _b_ _i_ _k_ _i_ e
8 b _o_ _a_ t
9 the u _n_ _d_ _e_ _r_ g _r_ _o_ _u_ _n_ d
10 t _r_ _a_ m
11 t _a_ _x_ i

B Complete what the people are saying with words from A.

1 I go to work by ...... _car_ ....

2 I go to work by ...... _train_ ....

3 I go to school by ...... _bike_ ....

4 I go to work by ...... _Taxi_ ....

5 I go to work by ...... _heli_ ....

6 I go to school by ...... _bus_ ....

20 In the town

A Circle the correct word in each pair.

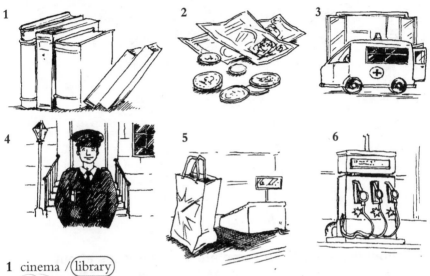

1 cinema / (library)
2 (bank) / post office
3 (hospital) / railway station
4 (police station) / tourist information office
5 restaurant / (shop)
6 (garage) / supermarket

B Complete the answers to the questions with the other words from A.

1 Where can I get something to eat?   At a _restaurant_ .
2 Where can I buy a train ticket?   At the _railway station_
3 Where can I buy stamps?   At the _post office_.
4 Where can I see a film?   At the _cinema_ .
5 Where can I do my shopping?   At a _shop_ .
6 Where can I get information about the town? At the _tourist infor office_

Test 2 (Units 11–20)

A What month is it and what is the weather like?

1 It's F*riday* .... 12 N*ovember* .... It's *foggy* ....

2 It's M*ONDAY* .... 25 F*EBRURY* .... It's *raining* ....

3 It's W*ednesday* ...... 7 D*ececembu* .... It's *raining* ....

4 It's Tu*esday* .... 29 S*eptembea* .... It's *windy* ....

5 It's Sa*turday* .... 13 O*ctober* .... It's *cloudy* ....

6 It's Th*ursday* .... 31 Au*gust* .... It's *sunny* ....

B Follow the lines. Then complete the sentences about where the people are going and how they are travelling.

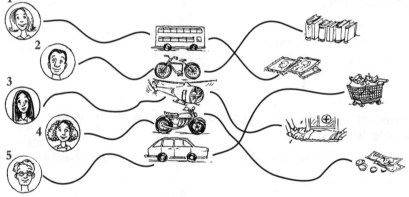

1 She's going to the *post office* . She's going by *bus* .

2 He's going to the *library* . He's going by *bike* .

3 She's going to *hospital* . She's *going by heli* .

4 She's going to the *bank* . She's *going by motorbike* .

5 He's going to the *supermarket* . He's *going by car* .

28

C Complete the sentences with words for rooms.

1 I sleep in the ....bed...........

2 I have a shower in the ....bathroom.... .

3 I eat in the ....kitchen......... . *dining room*

4 I watch TV in the ....living room....

5 I cook in the ....kitchen....... .

D Complete the crossword with the words for nine things from a house.

¹C	U	R	²T	A	I	N	S			
			O							
³S	H	O	W	E	R		⁴P			
			E				I			
	⁵A	L	A	R	⁶M	C	L	O	C	K
					I		L			
				R	O		⁷B			
	⁸M	I	C	R	O	W	A	V	E	
				O			D			
			⁹F	R	I	D	G	E		

1 things you put on a window to keep the light out
2 something you use to dry yourself
3 something you stand under to wash your body
4 something you put your head on when you go to sleep
5 something that wakes you up in the morning
6 something you look into to see yourself
7 something you lie on when you go to sleep
8 something you use to make food hot very quickly
9 something that keeps food cold

21 Jobs

A Find the words for twelve jobs in the grid. Then complete the words in the list below.

f	i	r	e	f	i	g	h	t	e	r	h	b
a	g	l	d	o	c	t	o	r	n	e	a	r
r	x	l	m	q	n	p	w	d	g	n	i	i
m	w	a	p	s	u	j	a	n	i	n	r	l
e	v	w	o	k	r	o	i	a	n	i	d	w
r	u	y	y	g	s	r	t	l	e	s	r	e
t	w	e	v	f	e	o	e	y	e	e	e	c
q	c	r	r	z	t	b	r	h	r	r	s	v
p	s	e	c	r	e	t	a	r	y	i	s	b
p	o	l	i	c	e	o	f	f	i	c	e	r
m	e	c	h	a	n	i	c	h	a	i	r	m
o	k	g	r	y	t	e	a	c	h	e	r	p

1 d*octor*
2 e*NGINEER*
3 f*ARMER*
4 f*IREFIGHTER*
5 h*AIRDRESSER*
6 l*AWYER*
7 m*ECHANIC*
8 n*URSE*
9 p*OLICE OFFICER*
10 s*ECRETARY*
11 t*EACHER*
12 w*AITER*

B Complete the sentences with the words from A.

1 I work in a hospital. I look after people who are ill. I'm a _____*nurse*_____ .

2 I give lessons in a school. I'm a *TEACHER* .

3 I design roads, bridges, machines, etc. I'm an *ENGINEER* .

4 I serve people in a restaurant. I'm a *WAITER* .

5 I advise people about the law. I'm a *lawyer* .

6 I work in an office, typing letters, etc. I'm a *secretary* .

7 I keep animals and grow food in the countryside. I'm a *farme* .

8 I cut people's hair. I'm a *hairdresser* .

9 I treat people who are ill. I'm a *doctor* .

10 I fix cars. I'm a *mechanic* .

11 I try to stop people doing bad things. I'm a *police officer* .

12 I put out fires. I'm a *fire fighter* .

22 Free time

A Complete the sentences with the words in the box.

cooking doing eating going for going for going to the
listening to playing ~~reading~~ watching

1 Julia likes ..... *reading* ..... books.

2 She likes ..... cooking ..... food.

3 She likes ..... watching ..... TV.

4 She likes ..... going to the ..... cinema.

5 She likes ..... going for ..... walks.

6 She likes ..... listening ..... music.

7 She likes ..... playing ..... the piano.

8 She likes ..... going ..... out.

9 She likes ..... going for ..... a run.

10 She likes ..... doing ..... aerobics.

23 Sports

A Put the letters in order. Then join the words with the pictures.

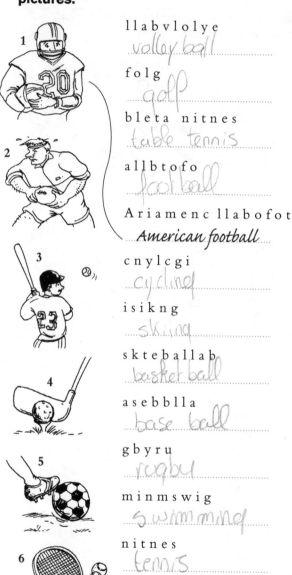

llabvlolye

volley ball

folg

golf

bleta nitnes

table tennis

allbtofo

football

Ariamenc llabofot

American football

cnylcgi

cycling

isikng

skiing

skteballab

basket ball

asebblla

base ball

gbyru

rugby

minmswig

swimming

nitnes

tennis

24 Animals

A Circle the correct word in each pair.

1 (chicken) / dog
2 bird / (cow)
3 cat / (duck)
4 fish / horse
5 pig / rabbit
6 mouse / sheep

B Complete the sentences with the other words from A.

1 I've got a .... *rabbit* ....   2 I've got a ....

3 I've got a ....   4 I've got a ....

5 I've got a ....   6 I've got a ....

25 Food and drink

A Match the words in the box with the pictures.

meat   fish   ~~fruit~~   vegetables

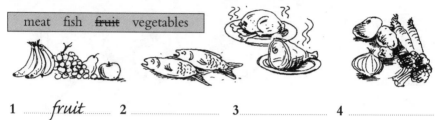

1 ....*fruit*....   2 ....   3 ....   4 ....

B Complete the crossword.

C Complete the sentences with the words in the box.

bread   pasta   rice

1 If you want to make sandwiches, remember to buy ....

2 It takes about 20 minutes to cook ....

3 If you want to make spaghetti bolognese, remember to buy ....

26 Food and menus

A Find the words for 10 types of food in the grid. Then complete the words in the list below.

h	a	m	b	u	r	g	e	r	a	i	r
s	a	i	r	e	w	h	t	s	b	c	c
s	l	p	i	z	z	a	e	h	r	e	h
a	c	z	g	e	r	y	i	n	i	c	o
n	h	c	a	k	e	l	w	s	a	r	c
d	i	h	d	n	a	x	q	d	m	e	o
w	p	b	i	s	c	u	i	t	s	a	l
i	s	p	a	w	v	c	z	l	h	m	a
c	t	s	u	d	e	t	c	m	j	f	t
h	r	e	t	s	n	e	r	a	k	f	e
k	n	f	e	d	c	r	i	s	p	s	j
m	z	h	o	t	d	o	g	b	p	x	l

1 h a m b u r g e r
2 p _ _ _ _
3 b _ _ _ _ _ _ _
4 c _ _ _
5 c _ _ _ _
6 s _ _ _ _ _ _ _
7 c _ _ _ _ _
8 c _ _ _ _ _ _ _ _
9 h _ _ d _ _
10 i _ _ _ _ _ _ _

B Complete the menu with words from A. Use some words more than once.

Menu

1 cheese ....sandwich....
2 ham ....
3 cheese & tomato ....
4 pepperoni ....
5 ....
6 ....
7 ....
8 vanilla ....
9 strawberry ....
10 chocolate ....
11 ....

27 Everyday verbs

A Complete the sentences with the words in the box.

> drinking eating playing reading
> washing ~~watching~~ wearing writing

1 He's *watching* TV.
2 She's .... the newspaper.
3 She's .... tennis.
4 He's .... a glass of milk.
5 He's .... his hands.
6 She's .... a letter.
7 He's .... an ice cream.
8 She's .... a big hat.

B Complete the sentences with the verbs in the box.

> listen sleep speak study talk ~~work~~

1 I ......*work*........ in an office.
2 I want to .... medicine at university.
3 How many languages can you .... ?
4 Would you like to .... to some music?
5 They're making too much noise. I can't ....
6 I don't want to .... about it.

28 Verbs of movement

A Put the letters in order.

1 klaw
   ...walk...

2 nur
   ....

3 pmuj
   ....

4 cande
   ....

5 lafl
   ....

6 blimc
   ....

7 misw
   ....

8 virde
   ....

9 dire
   ....

10 ckki
   ....

11 tis
   ....

12 danst
   ....

B The underlined words are in the wrong sentences. Write the correct word for each sentence.

1 He's <u>climbing</u> a car.   ...driving...

2 He's <u>driving</u> a ball.   ....

3 He's <u>falling</u> on a chair.   ....

4 He's <u>sitting</u> down the stairs.   ....

5 He's <u>kicking</u> a bike.   ....

6 He's <u>riding</u> a mountain.   ....

7 He's <u>dancing</u> in the sea.   ....

8 He's <u>swimming</u> to the music.   ....

29 Daily routine

A Write sentences with the phrases in the box. Remember to use the correct verb ending.

> have a shower   have breakfast   have lunch   get dressed
> get undressed   get up   go home   go to bed   go to sleep
> go to work   make dinner   ~~wake up~~

1 Joe *wakes up.*

2 He ....

3 ....

4 ....

5 ....

6 ....

7 ....

8 ....

9 ....

10 ....

11 ....

12 ....

30 Hello, Goodbye, etc.

A Match the words in the box with the pictures.

> Excuse me.　Fine, thank you.　Goodbye.　Good morning.
> Good night.　Hello.　Hi.　How do you do?　Sorry.
> ~~Thank you.~~　Yes, please.　You're welcome.

1 Thank you...

2

3 How are you?

4

5

6 Would you like one?

7

8

9

10 How do you do?

11

12 Thank you.

A What do the people do and what do they like doing in their free time? Complete the sentences.

1

I'm a *hairdresser* . In my free time I like ___*playing*___ football.

2

I'm a _____ . In my free time I like _____ .

3

I'm a _____ . In my free time I like _____ TV.

4

I'm a _____ . In my free time I like _____ for walks with my dog.

B Follow the lines. Then complete the sentences about what the people are having to eat and drink.

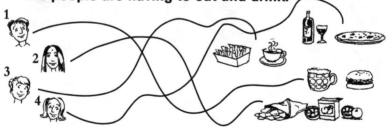

1 James is having _____*beer*_____ and a _____*hamburger*_____ .

2 Narinder is having _____ and _____ .

3 Henry is having _____ and _____ .

4 Sophie is having _____ and _____ .

C Complete the crossword with seven verbs.

1 you do this in a car
2 you do this on a bike or a horse
3 you do this at a party or a disco
4 you do this up a mountain
5 you do this in the water
6 you do this with your feet
7 you do this to a ball

D Put the four actions in each list in order. Which do you do first (1)? Which do you do last (4)?

I get dressed. ☐
I get up. ☐
I have a shower. ☐
I wake up. 1

I have lunch. ☐
I go home. ☐
I go to work. ☐
I make dinner. ☐

I get undressed. ☐
I go to bed. ☐
I go to sleep. ☐
I have a shower. ☐

E Join the pairs of sentences.

1 I'm going to bed now.
2 How do you do?
3 How are you?
4 Thank you for the present.
5 Hello, Karen.
6 You're sitting on my hat.

Hi, Robert.
You're welcome.
Good night.
Fine, thank you.
Sorry.
How do you do?

Answer Key

1 Your body

A 1 *foot*
2 neck
3 mouth
4 toe
5 face
6 hand
7 nose

B 1 *finger*
2 eye
3 head
4 arm
5 ear
6 hair
7 leg

2 Clothes

A 1 *trousers,*
shirt, jacket,
shoes
2 jeans, T-shirt
3 skirt, jumper
4 scarf, hat,
gloves, coat
5 dress

B 1 *jeans*
2 shoes
3 coat
4 gloves
5 scarf
6 trousers
7 hat

3 Describing character

A 1 *clever*
2 lazy
3 stupid
4 funny
5 unkind
6 shy
7 friendly
8 boring
9 naughty

B 1 *stupid*
2 unfriendly
3 good
4 kind

4 Describing appearance

A 1 *ugly*
2 thin
3 ugly
4 young
5 tall

B 1 *old*
2 fat
3 young
4 tall
5 beautiful
6 short
7 handsome
8 ugly

C 1 *long*
2 short
3 curly
4 straight

5 How you feel

A		B		C	
1	*tired*	1	*happy*	1	*bored*
2	thirsty	2	frightened	2	sad
3	ill	3	sad	3	frightened
4	hungry	4	bored	4	happy
5	cold	5	angry	5	angry
6	well				
7	hot				

6 The family

A women:
daughter,
granddaughter,
grandmother,
mother,
sister,
wife
men:
brother,
father,
grandfather,
grandson,
husband,
son

B		C	
1	*wife*	1	*father*
2	granddaughter	2	mother
3	husband	3	sister
4	sister	4	brother
5	father	5	grandmother
6	brother	6	grandfather
7	grandmother	7	wife
8	grandson	8	daughter
9	son	9	son
10	mother	10	husband
11	grandfather	11	granddaughter
12	daughter	12	grandson

7 Countries

Africa	*South Africa*
Asia	China, India, Japan
Australasia	Australia
Europe	France, Germany, Greece, Ireland, Italy, Poland, Portugal, Russia, Spain, Turkey, United Kingdom
North America	Canada, United States
South America	Argentina, Brazil

8 Nationalities and languages

nationalities	official languages
1 *Argentinian*	*Spanish*
2 Australian	English
3 Brazilian	Portuguese
4 Canadian	English + French
5 Chinese	Chinese
6 French	French
7 German	German
8 Greek	Greek
9 Indian	Hindi + English
10 Irish	Irish Gaelic + English
11 Italian	Italian
12 Japanese	Japanese
13 Polish	Polish
14 Portuguese	Portuguese
15 Russian	Russian
16 South African	English + Afrikaans
17 Spanish	Spanish
18 Turkish	Turkish
19 British	English
20 American	English

9 Numbers

A
a *3 three*
b 2 two
c 9 nine
d 6 six
e 0 zero
f 4 four
g 8 eight
h 1 one
i 10 ten
j 5 five
k 7 seven

B
e *11 eleven*
d 12 twelve
a 13 thirteen
j 14 fourteen
h 15 fifteen
f 16 sixteen
c 17 seventeen
i 18 eighteen
g 19 nineteen
b 20 twenty

C
1 *four*
2 seven
3 ten
4 twelve

10 Colours

A
1 *pink*
2 blue
3 brown
4 black
5 orange
6 green
7 yellow
8 white
9 grey
10 red

B
1 *yellow*
2 blue
3 white
4 green

C Students' own answers

Test 1 (Units 1–10)

A 1 hat, head
2 scarf, neck
3 gloves, hands
4 trousers, legs
5 shoes, feet

B 1 *mother, beautiful, dress*
2 grandmother, old, skirt, jumper
3 father, tall, trousers, shirt
4 sister, young, jeans, T-shirt

C 1 lazy
2 funny
3 kind
4 unkind
5 clever
6 boring

D 1 *hot*
2 ill
3 tired
4 bored
5 thirsty
6 frightened

E 1 *Argentinian*
2 France
3 Spanish
4 Japan
5 German
6 United States
7 Portugese
8 China

F a *seven*
b thirteen
c eighteen
d nine
e zero
f eleven
g fifteen
h one

G 1 *false: grey*
2 false: yellow
3 false: green
4 true
5 false: blue
6 true

11 Months of the year

A 1 *January*
2 February
3 March
4 April
5 May
6 June
7 July
8 August
9 September
10 October
11 November
12 December

B 1 *November*
2 October
3 January
4 December
5 February
6 September
7 May
8 June
9 August
10 April
11 March
12 July

12 Days of the week

A 1 *Monday*
2 Tuesday
3 Wednesday
4 Thursday
5 Friday
6 Saturday
7 Sunday

B 1 *Thursday*
2 Friday
3 Monday
4 Wednesday
5 Sunday
6 Tuesday
7 Saturday

13 The weather

A 1 *foggy*
 2 hot
 3 cloudy
 4 windy
 5 raining
 6 snowing
 7 sunny
 8 cold

B 1 *foggy*
 2 hot
 3 sunny
 4 raining
 5 cloudy
 6 windy
 7 snowing
 8 cold

14 A house

A 1 *bedrooms*
 2 bathroom
 3 living room
 4 dining room
 5 hall
 6 kitchen
 7 garden

B 1 *roof*
 2 window
 3 floor
 4 wall
 5 stairs
 6 door
 7 letterbox

15 Living room

A 1 *picture*
 2 light
 3 curtains
 4 CD player
 5 shelf
 6 sofa

B 7 *cushions*
 8 armchair
 9 rug
 10 table
 11 TV
 12 video

C a *armchair*
 b sofa
 c rug
 d shelf
 e picture
 f cushions

16 Kitchen

A 1 *fridge*
 2 sink
 3 cupboard
 4 washing machine
 5 cooker
 6 microwave

B 1 *glass*
 2 cup
 3 pan
 4 plate
 5 bowl
 6 knife
 7 spoon
 8 fork

17 Bathroom

A 1 *mirror*
 2 basin
 3 toilet
 4 bath
 5 shower

B 1 *toothbrush*
 2 soap
 3 toothpaste
 4 toilet paper
 5 towel
 6 shampoo

18 Bedroom

A
1 *pillow*
2 bed
3 sheet
4 duvet
5 alarm clock
6 lamp
7 chest of drawers
8 wardrobe

B
a *lamp*
b wardrobe
c bed
d duvet
e pillow
f alarm clock

19 Travel

A
1 *car*
2 train
3 bus
4 plane
5 helicopter
6 bike
7 motorbike
8 boat
9 the underground
10 tram
11 taxi

B
1 *car*
2 train
3 bike
4 taxi
5 helicopter
6 bus

20 In the town

A
1 *library*
2 bank
3 hospital
4 police station
5 shop
6 garage

B
1 *restaurant*
2 railway station
3 post office
4 cinema
5 supermarket
6 tourist information office

Test 2 (Units 11–20)

A
1 *Friday, November, foggy*
2 Monday, February, raining
3 Wednesday, December, snowing
4 Tuesday, September, windy
5 Saturday, October, cloudy
6 Thursday, August, sunny

B
1 *She's going to the post office. She's going by bus.*
2 He's going to the library. He's going by bike.
3 She's going to hospital. She's going by helicopter.
4 She's going to the bank. She's going by motorbike.
5 He's going to the supermarket. He's going by car.

C
1 bedroom
2 bathroom
3 dining room
4 living room
5 kitchen

D
1 curtains
2 towel
3 shower
4 pillow
5 alarm clock
6 mirror
7 bed
8 microwave
9 fridge

21 Jobs

A 1 *doctor*
   2 engineer
   3 farmer
   4 firefighter
   5 hairdresser
   6 lawyer
   7 mechanic
   8 nurse
   9 police officer
  10 secretary
  11 teacher
  12 waiter

B 1 *nurse*
   2 teacher
   3 engineer
   4 waiter
   5 lawyer
   6 secretary
   7 farmer
   8 hairdresser
   9 doctor
  10 mechanic
  11 police officer
  12 firefighter

22 Free time

A 1 *reading*
   2 cooking
   3 watching
   4 going to the
   5 going for
   6 listening to
   7 playing
   8 eating
   9 going for
  10 doing

23 Sports

A 1 *American football*
   2 rugby
   3 baseball
   4 golf
   5 football
   6 tennis
   7 basketball
   8 volleyball
   9 swimming
  10 cycling
  11 table tennis
  12 skiing

24 Animals

A 1 *chicken*
   2 cow
   3 duck
   4 horse
   5 pig
   6 sheep

B 1 *rabbit*
   2 bird
   3 dog
   4 cat
   5 fish
   6 mouse

25 Food and drink

A 1 *fruit*
   2 fish
   3 meat
   4 vegetables

B 1 *water*
   2 orange juice
   3 wine
   4 tea
   5 beer
   6 milk
   7 coffee

C 1 bread
   2 rice
   3 pasta

26 Food and menus

A 1 *hamburger*
   2 pizza
   3 biscuits
   4 cake
   5 chips
   6 sandwich
   7 crisps
   8 chocolate
   9 hot dog
   10 ice cream

B 1 *sandwich*
   2 sandwich
   3 pizza
   4 pizza
   5 hamburger
   6 hot dog
   7 chips
   8 ice cream
   9 ice cream
   10 cake
   11 crisps

27 Everyday verbs

A 1 *watching*
   2 reading
   3 playing
   4 drinking
   5 washing
   6 writing
   7 eating
   8 wearing

B 1 *work*
   2 study
   3 speak
   4 listen
   5 sleep
   6 talk

28 Verbs of movement

A 1 *walk*
   2 run
   3 jump
   4 dance
   5 fall
   6 climb
   7 swim
   8 drive
   9 ride
   10 kick
   11 sit
   12 stand

B 1 *driving*
   2 kicking
   3 sitting
   4 falling
   5 riding
   6 climbing
   7 swimming
   8 dancing

29 Daily routine

A 1 Joe *wakes up*.
   2 He gets up.
   3 He has a shower.
   4 He gets dressed.
   5 He has breakfast.
   6 He goes to work.
   7 He has lunch.
   8 He goes home.
   9 He makes dinner.
   10 He gets undressed.
   11 He goes to bed.
   12 He goes to sleep.

30 Hello, Goodbye, etc.

A
1 *Thank you.*
2 Excuse me.
3 Fine, thank you.
4 Hello.
5 Goodbye.
6 Yes, please.
7 Good morning.
8 Sorry.
9 Hi.
10 How do you do?
11 Good night.
12 You're welcome.

Test 3 (Units 21–30)

A
1 *hairdresser, playing*
2 teacher, reading
3 farmer, watching
4 secretary, going

B
1 *beer hamburger*
2 crisps, orange juice
3 chips, tea
4 wine, pizza

C
1 drive
2 ride
3 dance
4 climb
5 swim
6 walk
7 kick

D
I get dressed. 4
I get up. 2
I have a shower. 3
I wake up. *1*

I have lunch. 2
I go home. 3
I go to work. 1
I make dinner. 4

I get undressed. 1
I go to bed. 3
I go to sleep. 4
I have a shower. 2

E
1 Good night.
2 How do you do?
3 Fine, thank you.
4 You're welcome.
5 Hi, Robert.
6 Sorry.

Word List

The words in this list are British English. Sometimes we give you an important American English word which means the same.

1 Your body
arm /ɑːm/
ear /ɪər/
eye /aɪ/
face /feɪs/
finger /ˈfɪŋɡər/
foot /fʊt/ (plural = feet)
hair /heər/ (Use with a singular verb, e.g. Her hair *is* very long.)
hand /hænd/
head /hed/
leg /leɡ/
mouth /maʊθ/
neck /nek/
nose /nəʊz/
toe /təʊ/

2 Clothes
coat /kəʊt/
dress /dres/
gloves /ɡlʌvz/ (two gloves = a pair of gloves)
hat /hæt/
jacket /ˈdʒækɪt/
jeans /dʒiːnz/ (Use with a plural verb, e.g. His jeans *are* too short.)
jumper /ˈdʒʌmpər/ (US = sweater)
scarf /skɑːf/ (plural = scarves)
shirt /ʃɜːt/
shoes /ʃuːz/ (two shoes = a pair of shoes)
skirt /skɜːt/
trousers /ˈtraʊzəz/ (US usually = pants) (Use with a plural verb, e.g. Her trousers *are* red.)
T-shirt /ˈtiːʃɜːt/

3 Describing character

boring /ˈbɔːrɪŋ/
clever /ˈklevəʳ/
friendly /ˈfrendli/
funny /ˈfʌni/
good /gʊd/
kind /kaɪnd/
lazy /ˈleɪzi/
naughty /ˈnɔːti/
shy /ʃaɪ/
stupid /ˈstjuːpɪd/
unfriendly /ʌnˈfrendli/
unkind /ʌnˈkaɪnd/

4 Describing appearance

beautiful /ˈbjuːtɪfəl/
curly /ˈkɜːli/
fat /fæt/
handsome /ˈhændsəm/
long /lɒŋ/
old /əʊld/
short /ʃɔːt/
straight /streɪt/
tall /tɔːl/
thin /θɪn/
ugly /ˈʌgli/
young /jʌŋ/

5 How you feel

angry /'æŋgri/
bored /bɔːd/
cold /kəʊld/
frightened /'fraɪtənd/
happy /'hæpi/
hot /hɒt/
hungry /'hʌŋgri/
ill /ɪl/
sad /sæd/
thirsty /'θɜːsti/
tired /'taɪəd/
well /wel/

6 The family

brother /'brʌðər/
daughter /'dɔːtər/
father /'fɑːðər/(informal = dad)
granddaughter /'grænd͵dɔːtər/
grandfather /'grænd͵fɑːðər/ (informal = grandad)
grandmother /'grænd͵mʌðər/ (informal = grandma)
grandson /'grændsʌn/
husband /'hʌzbənd/
mother /'mʌðər/ (informal = mum; US informal = mom)
sister /'sɪstər/
son /sʌn/
wife /waɪf/

7 Countries

Argentina /ˌɑːdʒənˈtiːnə/
Australia /ɒsˈtreɪliə/
Brazil /brəˈzɪl/
Canada /ˈkænədə/
China /ˈtʃaɪnə/
France /frɑːnts/
Germany /ˈdʒɜːməni/
Greece /griːs/
India /ˈɪndiə/
Ireland /ˈaɪələnd/
Italy /ˈɪtəli/
Japan /dʒəˈpæn/
Poland /ˈpəʊlənd/
Portugal /ˈpɔːtʃəgəl/
Russia /ˈrʌʃə/
South Africa /ˌsaʊθ ˈæfrɪkə/
Spain /speɪn/
Turkey /ˈtɜːki/
United Kingdom /juːˈnaɪtɪd ˈkɪŋdəm/ (*also* UK = England, Scotland, Wales and Northern Ireland)
United States /juːˈnaɪtɪd ˈsteɪts/ (*also* USA)

8 Nationalities and languages

American /əˈmerɪkən/
Argentinian /ˌɑːdʒənˈtɪniən/
Australian /ɒsˈtreɪliən/
Brazilian /brəˈzɪliən/
British /ˈbrɪtɪʃ/
Canadian /kəˈneɪdiən/
Chinese /tʃaɪˈniːz/
French /frentʃ/
German /ˈdʒɜːmən/
Greek /griːk/

Indian /ˈɪndiən/
Irish /ˈaɪrɪʃ/
Italian /ɪˈtæliən/
Japanese /dʒæpəˈniːz/
Polish /ˈpəʊlɪʃ/
Portuguese /ˌpɔːtʃəˈgiːz/
Russian /ˈrʌʃən/
South African /ˌsaʊθ ˈæfrɪkən/
Spanish /ˈspænɪʃ/
Turkish /ˈtɜːkɪʃ/

9 Numbers

0 zero /ˈzɪərəʊ/
1 one /wʌn/
2 two /tuː/
3 three /θriː/
4 four /fɔːr/
5 five /faɪv/
6 six /sɪks/
7 seven /ˈsevən/
8 eight /eɪt/
9 nine /naɪn/
10 ten /ten/
11 eleven /ɪˈlevən/
12 twelve /twelv/
13 thirteen /ˌθɜːˈtiːn/
14 fourteen /ˌfɔːˈtiːn/
15 fifteen /ˌfɪfˈtiːn/
16 sixteen /ˌsɪksˈtiːn/
17 seventeen /ˌsevənˈtiːn/
18 eighteen /ˌeɪˈtiːn/
19 nineteen /ˌnaɪnˈtiːn/
20 twenty /ˈtwenti/

10 Colours
black /blæk/
blue /bluː/
brown /braʊn/
green /griːn/
grey /greɪ/
orange /ˈɒrɪndʒ/
pink /pɪŋk/
red /red/
yellow /ˈjeləʊ/
white /waɪt/

11 Months of the year
January /ˈdʒænjuəri/
February /ˈfebruəri/
March /mɑːtʃ/
April /ˈeɪprəl/
May /meɪ/
June /dʒuːn/
July /dʒuˈlaɪ/
August /ˈɔːgəst/
September /sepˈtembər/
October /ɒkˈtəʊbər/
November /nəʊˈvembər/
December /dɪˈsembər/

12 Days of the week
Monday /ˈmʌndeɪ/
Tuesday /ˈtjuːzdeɪ/
Wednesday /ˈwenzdeɪ/
Thursday /ˈθɜːzdeɪ/
Friday /ˈfraɪdeɪ/
Saturday /ˈsætədeɪ/
Sunday /ˈsʌndeɪ/

13 The weather

cloudy /'klaʊdi/
cold /kəʊld/
foggy /'fɒgi/
hot /hɒt/
rain /reɪn/
snow /snəʊ/
sunny /'sʌni/
windy /'wɪndi/

14 A house

bathroom /'bɑːθruːm/
bedroom /'bedruːm/
dining room /'daɪnɪŋ ˌruːm/
door /dɔːr/
floor /flɔːr/
garden /'gɑːdən/ (US = yard)
hall /hɔːl/
kitchen /'kɪtʃɪn/
letterbox /'letəbɒks/
living room /'lɪvɪŋ ˌruːm/
roof /ruːf/
stairs /steərz/
wall /wɔːl/
window /'wɪndəʊ/

15 Living room

armchair /ˈɑːmˌtʃeəʳ/
CD player /ˌsiːdi ˈpleɪəʳ/
curtains /ˈkɜːtənz/
cushions /ˈkʊʃənz/
light /laɪt/
picture /ˈpɪktʃəʳ/
rug /rʌg/
shelf /ʃelf/ (plural = shelves)
sofa /ˈsəʊfə/
table /ˈteɪbl/
TV /ˌtiːˈviː/ (*also* television)
video /ˈvɪdiəʊ/

16 Kitchen

bowl /bəʊl/
cooker /ˈkʊkəʳ/ (US = stove)
cup /kʌp/
cupboard /ˈkʌbəd/
fork /fɔːk/
fridge /frɪdʒ/
glass /glɑːs/
knife /naɪf/ (plural = knives)
microwave /ˈmaɪkrəʊweɪv/
pan /pæn/
plate /pleɪt/
sink /sɪŋk/
spoon /spuːn/
washing machine /ˈwɒʃɪŋ məˌʃiːn/

17 Bathroom

basin /ˈbeɪsən/ (US = sink)
bath /bɑːθ/ (US = bathtub)
mirror /ˈmɪrəʳ/

shampoo /ʃæm'puː/
shower /'ʃaʊəʳ/
soap /səʊp/
toilet /'tɔɪlɪt/
toilet paper /'tɔɪlɪt ˌpeɪpəʳ/
toothbrush /'tuːθbrʌʃ/
toothpaste /'tuːθpeɪst/
towel /taʊəl/

18 Bedroom
alarm clock /ə'lɑːm klɒk/
bed /bed/
chest of drawers /ˌtʃest əv 'drɔːz/ (US = bureau)
duvet /'duːveɪ/ (US = comforter)
lamp /læmp/
pillow /'pɪləʊ/
sheet /ʃiːt/
wardrobe /'wɔːdrəʊb/ (US = closet)

19 Travel
bike /baɪk/ (also bicycle)
boat /bəʊt/
bus /bʌs/
car /kɑːʳ/
helicopter /'helɪkɒptəʳ/
motorbike /'məʊtəbaɪk/
plane /pleɪn/ (also aeroplane; US = airplane)
taxi /'tæksi/
train /treɪn/
tram /træm/
underground /'ʌndəgraʊnd/ (US = subway)

20 In the town

bank /bæŋk/
cinema /ˈsɪnəmə/ (US = movie theater)
garage /ˈgærɑːʒ/
hospital /ˈhɒspɪtəl/
library /ˈlaɪbrəri/
police station /pəˈliːs ˌsteɪʃən/
post office /ˈpəʊst ˌɒfɪs/
railway station /ˈreɪlweɪ ˌsteɪʃən/
restaurant /ˈrestərɒnt/
shop /ʃɒp/
supermarket /ˈsuːpəmɑːkɪt/
tourist information office /ˈtʊərɪst ɪnfəˈmeɪʃən ˌɒfɪs/

21 Jobs

doctor /ˈdɒktər/
engineer /endʒɪˈnɪər/
farmer /ˈfɑːmər/
firefighter /ˈfaɪəfaɪtər/ (also fireman)
hairdresser /ˈheəˌdresər/
lawyer /ˈlɔɪər/
mechanic /mɪˈkænɪk/
nurse /nɜːs/
police officer /pəˈliːs ˌɒfɪsər/ (also policeman/policewoman)
secretary /ˈsekrətˌri/
teacher /ˈtiːtʃər/
waiter /ˈweɪtər/ (female waiter = waitress)

22 Free time

doing aerobics /ˌduːɪŋ eəˈrəʊbɪks/
cooking /ˈkʊkɪŋ/
eating out /ˌiːtɪŋ ˈaʊt/
going for a run /ˌgəʊɪŋ fər ə ˈrʌn/
going for walks /ˌgəʊɪŋ fə ˈwɔːks/

going to the cinema /ˌgəʊɪŋ tə ðə ˈsɪnəmə/ (US = going to the movies)
listening to music /ˌlɪsənɪŋ tə ˈmjuːzɪk/
playing the piano /ˌpleɪɪŋ ðə piˈaenəʊ/
reading /ˈriːdɪŋ/
watching TV /ˌwɒtʃɪŋ tiːˈviː/

23 Sports
American football /əˌmerɪkən ˈfʊtbɔːl/ (US = football)
baseball /ˈbeɪsbɔːl/
basketball /ˈbɑːskɪtbɔːl/
cycling /ˈsaɪklɪŋ/
football /ˈfʊtbɔːl/ (US = soccer)
golf /gɒlf/
rugby /ˈrʌgbi/
skiing /ˈskiːɪŋ/
swimming /ˈswɪmɪŋ/
table tennis /ˈteɪbl ˌtenɪs/
tennis /ˈtenɪs/
volleyball /ˈvɒlibɔːl/

24 Animals
bird /bɜːd/
cat /kæt/
chicken /ˈtʃɪkɪn/
cow /kaʊ/
dog /dɒg/
duck /dʌk/
fish /fɪʃ/ (plural = fish)
horse /hɔːs/
mouse /maʊs/ (plural = mice)
pig /pɪg/
rabbit /ˈræbɪt/
sheep /ʃiːp/ (plural = sheep)

25 Food and drink

beer /bɪəʳ/

bread /bred/

coffee /ˈkɒfi/

fish /fɪʃ/

fruit /fruːt/

meat /miːt/

milk /mɪlk/

orange juice /ˈɒrɪndʒ ˌdʒuːs/

pasta /ˈpæstə/

rice /raɪs/

tea /tiː/

vegetables /ˈvedʒtəblz/

water /ˈwɔːtəʳ/

wine /waɪn/

26 Food and menus

biscuits /ˈbɪskɪts/ (US = cookies)

cake /keɪk/

chips /tʃɪps/ (US = French fries)

chocolate /ˈtʃɒkələt/

crisps /krɪsps/ (US = chips)

hamburger /ˈhæmˌbɜːgəʳ/

hot dog /ˈhɒt ˌdɒg/

ice cream /ˌaɪs ˈkriːm/

pizza /ˈpiːtsə/

sandwich /ˈsænwɪdʒ/

27 Everyday verbs

drink /drɪŋk/ (*past tense* drank; *past participle* drunk)
eat /iːt/ (*past tense* ate; *past participle* eaten)
listen /ˈlɪsən/
play /pleɪ/
read /riːd/ (*past tense* & *past participle* read)
sleep /sliːp/ (*past tense* & *past participle* slept)
speak /spiːk/ (*past tense* spoke; *past participle* spoken)
study /ˈstʌdi/
talk /tɔːk/
wash /wɒʃ/
watch /wɒtʃ/
wear /weər/ (*past tense* wore; *past participle* worn)
work /wɜːk/
write /raɪt/ (*past tense* wrote; *past participle* written)

28 Verbs of movement

climb /klaɪm/
dance /dɑːnts/
drive /draɪv/ (*past tense* drove; *past participle* driven)
fall /fɔːl/ (*past tense* fell; *past participle* fallen)
jump /dʒʌmp/
kick /kɪk/
ride /raɪd/ (*past tense* rode; *past participle* ridden)
run /rʌn/ (*past tense* ran; *past participle* run)
sit /sɪt/ (*past tense* & *past participle* sat)
stand /stænd/ (*past tense* & *past participle* stood)
swim /swɪm/ (*past tense* swam; *past participle* swum)
walk /wɔːk/

29 Daily routine

get dressed /ˌget ˈdrest/
get undressed /ˌget ʌnˈdrest/
get up /ˌget ˈʌp/
go home /ˌgəʊ ˈhəʊm/
go to bed /ˌgəʊ tə ˈbed/
go to sleep /ˌgəʊ tə ˈsliːp/
go to work /ˌgəʊ tə ˈwɜːk/
have a shower /ˌhæv ə ˈʃaʊər/
have breakfast /ˌhæv ˈbrekfəst/
have lunch /ˌhæv ˈlʌntʃ/
make dinner /ˌmeɪk ˈdɪnər/
wake up /ˌweɪk ˈʌp/

30 Hello, Goodbye, etc.

Excuse me /ɪkˈskjuːs ˌmiː/
Fine, thank you. /ˈfaɪn ˌθæŋk juː/
Goodbye /gʊdˈbaɪ/
Good morning /gʊd ˈmɔːnɪŋ/
Good night /gʊd ˈnaɪt/
Hello /helˈəʊ/
Hi /haɪ/ (informal)
How are you? /ˌhaʊ ˈɑːr juː/
How do you do? /ˌhaʊ djə ˈduː/ (formal)
Yes, please /ˈjes ˌpliːz/
Sorry /ˈsɒri/
Thank you /ˈθæŋk juː/
You're welcome /jɔː ˈwelkəm/